Best-Ever Circle Time Activities: Month by Month

50 Instant & Engaging Morning Meeting Activities & Games That Build Skills All Year Long!

by Ellen Booth Church
With Linda Perline

SCHOLASTIC
PROFESSIONAL BOOKS

NEW YORK • TORONTO • LONDON • AUCKLAND • SYDNEY
MEXICO CITY • NEW DELHI • HONG KONG • BUENOS AIRES

For Linda Perline, kindergarten teacher extraordinaire,
whose lifelong passion for teaching shines through the children she teaches
and her work on this book. Thank You.

A special thanks to Min Hong's first-graders:
Sarah, Christopher, Clarke, and Katherine

Cover photograph by Jimmy Levin
Cover design by Josué Castilleja
Interior design by Solutions by Design, Inc.
Interior illustrations by James Graham Hale

ISBN: 0-439-31662-6

1 2 3 4 5 6 7 8 9 10   40   08 07 06 05 04 03 02

Contents

Introduction

"Our task must be to free ourselves...by widening our circle of compassion to embrace all living creatures and the whole of nature and its beauty."
—Albert Einstein

What is it about circles? Is it that they have no beginning or end? That they are a container, yet, if considered as a line, they are infinite? Humans have always been drawn to the shape of the circle. Gather a group of people together in a conversation, and you'll usually see them naturally forming a circle!

There is something innate in circles, and so it makes sense that we use this shape (or that of an oval, depending on your space!) as the container within which we share thoughts and feelings. Circle time in our classrooms is a time when we gather children together in the safe haven of the circle—where all are equally accepted, appreciated, and heard.

How to Make the Most of Circle Time

Is circle time the joy of your day? It can be! It's the magical part of the day when you have the whole group together. There they are: smiling, wiggling, and ready to go. So what are you going to do? The first trick is to plan ahead and practice. The night before you're going to do an activity, read through it. If possible, practice the song or rhyme. That way, when you get to circle time you won't need to read from the book. (Young children tend to notice your eyes; eye contact is often key to children's attention!)

You'll also want to watch children's reactions. If you are losing them—going too long or doing something that is just not working—STOP! Don't worry about completing the activity or lesson plan, just use your keen sense of children and find a positive way to end the activity. Sing a quick song, do a fingerplay, say "The End"—whatever you can do to gracefully finish the activity and move on to something else.

Many of the activities in this book can and should be done several times. Don't think that you have to do every variation in one day or even one week! Revisit the activities frequently, changing one aspect now and then—and always go back to earlier activities at the end of the year.

If children exhibit behavior problems, look at what you're doing or asking them to do. Much of the misbehavior during circle time occurs because activities are either too long or developmentally inappropriate. Look to see if you are engaging the children enough. Together, create circle time rules for happy and cooperative gatherings.

Remember, this is a time for children to shine. Celebrate each child as well as the group you create together. Listen and share. You will be creating a community of learning that will last all year long!

Top-Ten Tips for the Best Circle Times Ever

- ⦿ Start with short-and-sweet circle times, and extend them over the course of the year. End short and sweet again!

- ⦿ Keep things interactive; be sure children have a say in the events of circle time.

- ⦿ Make activities multisensory. Children participate and understand better when they have something to see, hear, touch, even taste and smell!

- ⦿ Use surprise to get children's attention. Change the subject, do a quick song, make a silly noise—anything that gets them looking at you. Once you have children's attention, continue with the activity you had in mind.

- ⦿ Remember to apply humor liberally to your gatherings!

- ⦿ "Play dumb"! Children love to correct you, and in the process they will be learning to express their own knowledge of the topic.

- ⦿ Allow children to come to the circle when they are ready. Give them something else to do while others participate.

- ⦿ Get going! There will always be children who, for whatever reason, are not quite ready to sit down. Don't hold up the others. Dive in—children who are reluctant will usually join in once you start.

- ⦿ Invite children to lead circle time, too. They can lead a discussion, ask questions, and so on.

- ⦿ Create a safe environment for children to express not only their thoughts but also their feelings. Accept all children's ideas and feelings compassionately and equally.

Using This Book

Here's what you'll find on each page:

Curriculum Areas
The activities in this book cover a range of curriculum areas: Language and Literacy, Music and Movement, Science, Math, and Community Building.

Month
You'll find five or more activities for each month of the school year.

Materials List
Many of the activities in this book require no materials at all; when they do, they're listed here.

How-To
Simple step-by-step instructions let you know how to make the activity happen.

Skills
This list tells you which skills you're developing during your circle time.

Tips
You'll find plenty of ways to simplify, extend, or enrich the activity.

Using Chart Paper
Many of the activities include a suggestion for using chart paper as part of circle time (to record ideas, create graphs, and so on).

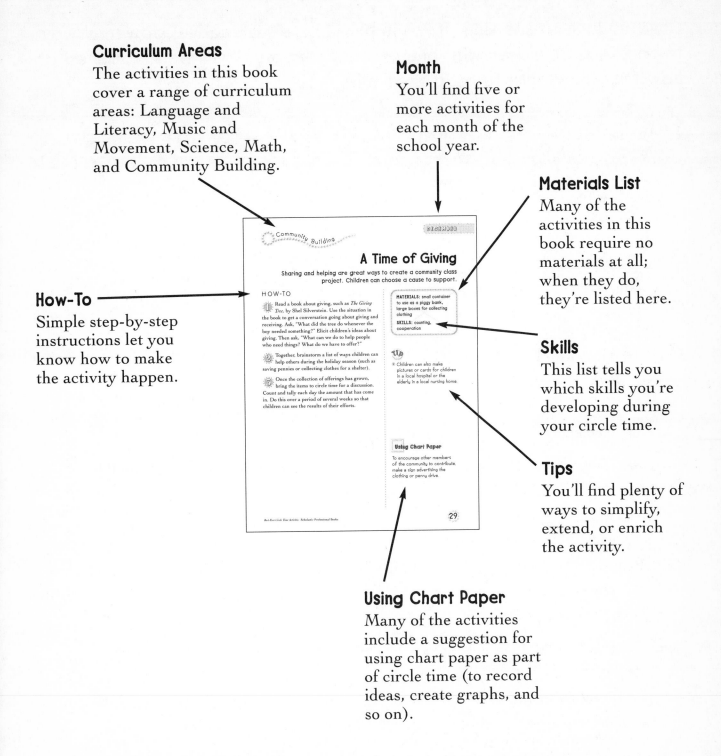

A Time of Giving
Sharing and helping are great ways to create a community class project. Children can choose a cause to support.

HOW-TO

Read a book about giving, such as *The Giving Tree*, by Shel Silverstein. Use the situation in the book to get a conversation going about giving and receiving. Ask, "What did the tree do whenever the boy needed something?" Elicit children's ideas about giving. Then ask, "What can we do to help people who need things? What do we have to offer?"

Together, brainstorm a list of ways children can help others during the holiday season (such as saving pennies or collecting clothes for a shelter).

Once the collection of offerings has grown, bring the items to circle time for a discussion. Count and tally each day the amount that has come in. Do this over a period of several weeks so that children can see the results of their efforts.

MATERIALS: small container to use as a piggy bank, large boxes for collecting clothing

SKILLS: counting, cooperation

Children can also make pictures or cards for children in a local hospital or the elderly in a local nursing home.

Using Chart Paper
To encourage other members of the community to contribute, make a sign advertising the clothing or penny drive.

Come Back and Play!

Children love to see their name in print. Here's an active, powerful way to familiarize children with one another's names. You'll be astonished at how fast they learn to read them all!

> **MATERIALS:** 2 identical sets of index cards with names of each child (include yourself)
>
> **SKILLS:** name recognition, receptive and expressive language

HOW-TO

1 Give each child his or her own name card. Begin with your aide or another adult in the room. Sing the following song to the tune of "Where Is Thumbkin?" Hold up one name card and sing:

> *Where is [name]?*
> *Where is [name]?*

2 That child stands up, holds up his or her name card, and says:

> *Here I am. Here I am.*

Then sing:

> *[Name], how are you?*
> *We are glad to see you.*
> *Run away, run away!*

That child runs away.

3 Enlist children's help in bringing the child back. Together, sing:

> *Come back and play!*
> *Come back and play!*

4 Ask for a volunteer to go next.

Tips

● You might establish that running is only allowed in the classroom during this game.

● Display children's names all around the room—on a sharing chart, snack chart, helpers chart, birthday chart, lost tooth chart, animal care chart, and so on. Encourage children to "read around the room" during choice time. Give several children pointers and let them go around the room, reading all the names they can. They will delight in finding their name and the names of their friends. (You might first demonstrate the safe use of pointers in reading the charts.)

Music & Movement

We Need You!

A friendly way to bring children to the rug is with a song.

HOW-TO

1 Tell children that by the end of the song they are about to sing, they should be sitting in a circle on the rug.

2 Begin the song and invite children to join in. Sing through two times (to the tune of "Here We Go 'Round the Mulberry Bush"):

> *Everybody on the rug, on the rug, on the rug.*
> *Everybody on the rug,*
> *For our circle time.*

MATERIALS: none

SKILLS: listening, following directions

 Tips

⦿ Bringing children to the rug in a positive way sets the tone and creates an enjoyable circle time experience.

⦿ This song can also be used to bring children together on the rug at other times during the day—for example, sharing time, calendar time, snack time, morning meeting.

Music & Movement

To the Rug!

Children need a reminder when it's almost time to change activities. This song is a fun and pleasant way to let them know that it's time to stop and join circle time.

HOW-TO

1. Tell children they should be sitting on the rug in a circle by the end of the song.

2. Begin the song and invite children to join in. Sing to the tune of "Frère Jacques":

   Morning meeting, morning meeting,
   On the rug, on the rug.
   Everybody come, everybody come,
   To the rug, to the rug.

MATERIALS: none

SKILLS: listening, following directions

Tips

⊙ If someone does not respond to the song, you can enlist the group's help in singing it one more time.

⊙ You can substitute the words *circle time* for *morning meeting.*

⊙ Another variation on this theme is "Bottoms on the Rug!" Sing to the tune of "If You're Happy and You Know It":

   Put your bottom on the rug,
   on the rug,
   Put your bottom on the rug,
   on the rug,
   Put your bottom on the rug
   and give yourself a hug,
   Put your bottom on the rug,
   on the rug.

Beginning Our Day

Here's another great way to welcome children to circle time.

HOW-TO

1 Have children sit in a circle and put their arms on each other's shoulders (explain that hands should not be on necks, only on shoulders). Invite children to sway gently as they sing the familiar song:

The more we get together, together, together,

The more we get together, the happier we'll be.

For your friends are my friends,

And my friends are your friends.

The more we get together, the happier we'll be.

2 After the song, start the greeting by turning to the child on your right and saying "Good morning, _____," and shaking his or her hand. That child says "Good morning" back and then turns to the child sitting to his or her right and continues the same greeting around the circle: "Good morning, _____." Everyone stays seated and children greet each other, all the way around the circle, until the greeting comes back to you.

MATERIALS: none

SKILLS: cooperation, communication, manners

- Model and role-play the importance of a firm but gentle handshake and appropriate eye contact during the greeting. You might do this every day for the first few weeks of the year to help children learn to listen to and respect one another.

- Explain to children what to do if they forget someone's name. They can whisper to the next child, "What is your name?"

- Instead of a handshake, use other greetings such as high or low five, high or low "pinkie touching," right elbows touching, right foot touching.

Day by Day

Here's a concrete, yearlong activity for keeping track of all the days you are in school.

HOW-TO

1 At each circle time, use a straw to record the day. Place the ones container in the chalk tray so that there is room above it to write a number. Each day, place one straw in the container and write the number above it.

2 On the tenth day, bring out the tens container and place it next to the ones container. Explain the rule: Whenever there are more than nine straws in the container, bundle the straws and put them in the next container, which holds bundles of ten.

3 On the ninety-ninth day, bring out the hundreds container and place it next to the tens container. Explain that whenever there are more than nine bundles in the container, we put them together and place them in the hundreds container.

> **MATERIALS:** 3 containers of different sizes (label the largest one "Hundreds," the medium-sized one "Tens" and the smallest one "Ones"), collection of straws, rubber bands, chalk
>
> **SKILLS:** counting, numeration, recording

- When adding a new straw each day, ask questions such as: "How many straws did we have yesterday? If we put one in today, how many do you think we will have? If we had three straws and we put one in, how many do you think we will have?" After predictions are made, count together to check.

- As you write the numbers above the containers, describe the formation of the number. Have children use a finger to write it in the air, on their hand, on the rug, or on the back of the child sitting next to them.

 Math

Straps or Shoelaces?

This is an active and fun way to introduce graphs.

HOW-TO

1 Ask everyone to take off one shoe and place it in the middle of the circle. Ask, "What do you notice about this pile of shoes?" Accept all answers.

2 Help children notice that some have shoelaces and others do not. Ask which there are more of. (Children will find it hard to tell.) You can offer a solution by starting two rows in the center of the circle and having everyone takes turns putting his or her shoe in the appropriate row.

3 When finished, explain that children have made a graph, which makes it easier to compare the shoes.

MATERIALS: none

SKILLS: classifying, sorting, graphing

 Tips

- Reproduce the graph on chart paper. Ask, "What do you notice? Which has more? Which has less? How many are there all together?"

- Invite children to form lines behind a toy car, bus, or person, to create a human graph that shows how they come to school.

Take Circle Time Outside!

The best way to learn about nature is to experience it with all your senses on a walk outdoors!

MATERIALS: none

SKILLS: sensory awareness, listening, speaking

HOW-TO

1 Have a discussion to define boundaries and set guidelines for behavior while outside. (It is best to have another adult along.)

2 On your nature walk, ask questions to channel children's natural curiosity. "What do you hear? What do you see? Look up, look down...what do you see now? What do you feel?" Continue as long as children maintain interest, then gather children into a circle.

3 Using a quiet, calm voice to help children get still and focused. Ask them to close their eyes, sit very still, and just listen. When they hear a sound, they should raise their hand. Call on children one at a time to tell what they hear.

Tips

⊙ Establish a "no running" rule until after circle time. Then you might ask children to hop like a rabbit, jump like a grasshopper, run like the wind, or slither like a snake.

⊙ At some point you may need to refocus the group. Try having them lay down and close their eyes.

Using Chart Paper

Back in the classroom, bring children into a circle and ask everyone to share something they saw or heard on the nature walk. Write all comments on a chart. Cut the sentences apart and glue each to the bottom of a large sheet of paper to make a class big book, and let children illustrate the pages. Place the book in the science corner or near your looking table!

14

Morning Message

A written message from you to the class is a great way to let children know you care and think about them. Read the message together during circle time.

HOW-TO

1 Write a simple message on chart paper, such as:

Good morning children.
Today is Monday. It is Rami's birthday!
We will learn a new game today!
Love, Mrs. Perline

2 Point to each word as you read aloud. Have the message in the same place every day. Change it slightly but repeat many of the same words for at least the first month, so that children are able to read it themselves. Bring attention to concepts of print by asking questions, such as "Where do we start when we begin reading? Who can find the letter t? The letter ∂? A period? How many words are in the first sentence? Who can come and point while we count together? How many letters are in this word?"

MATERIALS: chart paper, markers

SKILLS: expressive language, reading and writing skills

Tips

- Try to include one child's name each day in the message. ("Johnny is the line leader today; Jimmy is the caboose today; It is Kate's birthday.")

- Save daily messages. When everyone's name has been mentioned, staple the pages together for a Morning Message Book. Add it to your library so that children can decorate each page and read it again and again.

Come On, Children!

This is a wonderful activity to "get the wiggles out" so that children can sit still and refocus. Make it fun by doing silly movements!

HOW-TO

Sing the following song to the tune of "Mary Had a Little Lamb," while doing various hand or body movements for children to imitate (hands raised up high, hands to the side, one hand up and one hand down, wiggle and shake all over, slide to the side, march around the room, touch your toes, jump up, kick in place, clap your hands, run in place, snap your fingers, and so on).

Come on children, do this, do this, [demonstrate a movement]

Come on children, do this, do this,

Come on children, do this, do this,

Children, look at me!

Come on children turn around, turn around, turn around,

Come on children turn around,

Children, follow me!

MATERIALS: none

SKILLS: gross motor, listening, following directions

● You can use this same song at other times during the day (line up, cleanup and other transitions).

Using Chart Paper

Write the song on chart paper in large letters. Model pointing to the words while everyone reads together. Use chopsticks as pointers, and let children take turns!

 Music & Movement

Fire Safety Month

October is Fire Safety Month—enrich children's learning with a song!

HOW-TO

 1 With children, sing this song to the tune of "Frère Jacques":

Firefighter, firefighter,
You are brave, you are brave.
Putting out the fires, putting out the fires.
Lives you save, lives you save.

 2 Let children make up hand and body movements, or introduce the following signs in American sign language:

fire: curved open hands, fingers separated, palms facing in, "flutter" your fingers

fighter: make hands into fists, cross hands in front of body

you: point index finger outward

are: make an *r* in sign language (cross your index and middle finger and keep your thumb, pinky, and ring finger down, then place your hand on your lips and move it forward

brave: hold up both arms as if showing off muscles

putting out the fires: hold hands and arms as if holding a fire hose and move them back and forth

MATERIALS: none

SKILLS: fine motor, gross motor, listening

 Tip

⊚ Try another song, this one to the tune of "I'm a Little Tea Pot":

I'm a little firefighter dressed in red.
With a fire hat on my head
I can drive a fire truck, fight fires, too!
And make it safe for me and you!

Using Chart Paper

Visit a local fire station. Before the visit, ask, "What do you think you will see at the fire station?" Write all responses in one column of a chart. After your visit, ask, "What did you see at the fire station?" and record responses in the second column. Read and compare both lists.

Roll-a-Ball Greeting

Help children learn friendly greetings as they develop gross-motor coordination.

HOW-TO

1 Children can take turns greeting each other by rolling a ball! One child takes the ball and says, "Good morning, [child's name]," and then rolls the ball to another child in the circle. The "catcher" then says good morning to someone else and rolls the ball to him or her.

2 If necessary, discuss reasons for only one person catching the ball at a time. Remind children to roll the ball to someone who has not had a turn. In the middle of the game, you might ask anyone who has not had a turn to put his or her thumb up. Continue until each child has been greeted.

MATERIALS: ball

SKILLS: gross motor, greeting, listening

Using Chart Paper

Ask children what they believe their classroom should feel and look like (responses might include happy, cooperative, fair, friendly, everyone being included, people using nice voices, helping each other, working and playing together). Write it all down on chart paper and have everyone sign it. Tell them that they have created a belief statement and it is up to everyone who signed it to try to make it happen.

 Math

Five and Back

Here is a fun way to move around—and practice counting, too.

HOW-TO

1 Begin by having children sit on the rug. As you count aloud from zero to five, have children rise to their feet.

2 Start at five and slowly count backward to zero. By the time you reach zero, children should again be sitting on the rug. Repeat several times.

3 Gradually work your way up to ten.

4 Try these variations:

Ask for predictions ("How will your body look at 3, 5, 1...")

Count in a different language.

Count to 50 by tens.

Let a child lead the activity.

MATERIALS: none

SKILLS: counting forward and backward, one-to-one correspondence

 Tip

● Try a variation called 1-2-3-4 Jump. Sitting in a circle, children count off, going around the circle (1-2-3-4, 1-2-3-4). Instead of saying the number 5, the child whose turn it is says "Jump!" and jumps up (and stays standing up). The game continues until everyone in the circle is standing.

Season Scientists

What do scientists do? Ask children what they think!

HOW-TO

1 Ask children to tell you what they think scientists do. Accept all comments and write them down. Try to elicit the following: Scientists make predictions, ask questions, use all the senses to find answers to questions, and record what they learn.

2 Tell children that today they will be scientists and their question will be "What does fall look like where we live?" Give children each a small bag and a magnifying glass and tell them to go outside, explore, and bring back anything that will help answer the question. Back inside, gather children in a circle. Each child places one object on a tray in the middle of the circle.

3 Ask, "What did you see on our walk?" (Observations need not be limited to the objects on the tray.) Write the responses on a chart and read it together after everyone has contributed.

MATERIALS: small bag and plastic magnifying glass (1 per child, tray)

SKILLS: observing, descriptive language

- Make a class collage using the found objects. You might label the objects as well, giving the students a rich fall vocabulary.

- Sort the items by color, size, shape, and material.

- Turn children's responses into a book to illustrate, and place it in the science corner.

Science

Leaf Hunt

Invite children to find and compare leaves.

HOW-TO

1. Give each child a small bag and go outside with the goal of collecting leaves.

2. Come back inside and empty all the bags into a pile in the middle of the circle. Ask, "What do you see? How can we sort the leaves?" (by size, shape, color, and so on) Decide together what attribute will be used for sorting and then begin, giving everyone a chance to put a leaf into a group.

3. Challenge children to repeat the exercise, this time grouping the leaves a different way.

MATERIALS: small bag (1 per child)

SKILLS: observing, sorting, classifying

 Tips

◉ Make a labeled leaf book with real or drawn leaves, and place it in the science corner.

◉ Crayon rubbings of leaves can be used to decorate the room.

◉ Use a magnifying glass to look more closely at the veins in the leaves and compare them to the veins in your hands and wrists.

Using Chart Paper

Graph the leaves into two categories: big or little, fat or skinny, bumpy or smooth, and so on. Ask for predictions and observations during the graphing process.

The Museum of Me

Celebrate children one by one—and get all kids talking and sharing about themselves and their families.

HOW-TO

1 Choose one child at a time to be the curator of the "Me Museum." Send home a note in advance to explain the process. Encourage families to send in family photos as well as a favorite toy, game, book—even a favorite food!

2 At circle time, invite the child to show the items. You might ask questions, such as "What are you doing in this photo? Why is this your favorite toy? What do you like to do with it?" You'll be modeling good question formation for the other children, an essential part of language development. Encourage the rest of the group to ask questions, too.

3 After circle time, set up a table to display the museum pieces. The child can act as curator and meet and share his treasures with visitors during choice time.

Using Chart Paper

Children can interview the curator with a pretend microphone made out of a paper towel tube stuffed with a ball of foil. They might ask questions, such as "What is your favorite food? Color? Game? Breakfast food?" Record on a chart with the child's name at the top and the questions and answers listed below. Hang it in the "Me Museum" for the week!

> **MATERIALS:** children's favorite photos and objects (brought in from home), poster paper
>
> **SKILLS:** expressive and receptive language, self-concept

- Children need lots of opportunities to practice sharing. Of course, the hardest things to share are favorite treasures! When sharing is put in the context of a museum, it shifts the child's experience to a purposeful and positive one.

- Don't panic if no photos come in from home…take some with an instant camera!

- Read aloud one of the favorite books from the "Me Museum" at story time.

Music & Movement

Do as I Say...Not as I Do!

Here is a new twist on the traditional Simon Says. Children listen and follow directions without being confused by what the leader is doing.

HOW-TO

1 As the leader, give directions for children to follow. Children must do only what you say, not what you do! For instance, you might say, "Touch your head!" as you are touching your knee.

2 Remind children that it takes a lot of concentration and attention to be able to respond to only spoken directions. Children who are very visual may have to work extra hard to follow your directions, but it is great practice for all.

3 Later, children might enjoy leading this game.

MATERIALS: none

SKILLS: listening, following directions, coordination

 TIPS

◉ You can start the game by having children play with their eyes closed. This helps them learn to focus on your directions. Eventually, have children open their eyes and play the game.

◉ This is a great one for getting children focused for a more serious circle time activity!

Community Building

Show-and-Tell With a Twist

Competitiveness can sometimes occur among children during show and tell. On the other hand, it can be a great opportunity for children to talk in front of the group. Try some of these fresh approaches.

Show-and-Tell "Homework"

Give children theme-related guidelines for choosing an object to bring to school. For example, for your shape unit they can bring in something round; during your family unit it can be a family photo! The commonality among these objects will encourage more focused conversations.

Show-and-Share

Children are often afraid that their objects will get broken or lost when they are passed around the circle. Set up a show-and-share table in your circle time area so that children can safely share their special object under their own watchful eyes! Children can also show and share intangibles, such as a new song, a joke, or the ability to snap their fingers!

Show-and-Tell Riddles

Invite children to look for an object to bring to school the next day. Ask them to put the object in a bag so no one can see it. Then have them think of a riddle to help the other children guess what it is, such as "It's blue and round and you bounce it." (*a ball*)

> **MATERIALS:** objects children bring in from home
>
> **SKILLS:** listening, descriptive language, speaking in front of a group

- Be sensitive to children in the class who do not have many choices of objects to bring from home. Help them understand that whatever they have chosen is special.

- Talk to families about your approach to show-and-tell. It is important that they understand that this is not a "show off" situation in which their family will be judged.

 Math

Patterns of People

The concept of patterning is essential for math processing because counting, and eventually equations, are both types of patterning. This activity physically involves children in a pattern sequence.

HOW-TO

1 Invite three or four children to volunteer to be part of a line pattern. Ask one child to stand and the next to sit. Invite the other children in the group to "read" the pattern (describing a pattern helps deepen children's understanding).

2 Request a volunteer to add him or herself to the pattern, asking, "Who wants to be in the pattern? Will you stand or sit?" One by one, children add to the pattern. When the line is full, the children can "sound off" the pattern by saying their placement (standing, sitting) as you point down the line.

3 Now do it another way! Ask, "What is another way we can use ourselves to make a line pattern?" Other pattern options include boy-girl, front-back, hands up-hands down, clothing color, different facial expressions, and so on.

Using Chart Paper

Visual patterns have a rhythm of their own. Display simple pictures or drawings to create a pattern—for example, pear, pear, apple, pear, pear, apple. Add claps for the syllables of the words and you have a great rhythm section!

MATERIALS: none

SKILLS: observing, sequencing, classifying

- Stick to simple ABAB patterns at first. Later, add more complexity, such as ABCABC or ABBA.

- Reverse and expand the thinking process by having a few children line themselves up in a pattern for the others to guess!

- Integrate your themes into the pattern. Children can stand in line holding crayons when learning about colors or pictures of animals during your animal unit.

Learning About Time

Children might want to know if it is time to go home just when you sit down for morning meeting! Help children develop an understanding of time by marking it off in familiar sequences.

HOW-TO

1 Take photos throughout the day. Record every separate activity from arrival to departure—circle time, snack, story, and choice time, and so on.

2 At circle time, invite children to help you sort the photos into a sequence from first event of the day to last. Talk about what you do at each time. Using a glue stick, have children paste each picture onto a long strip of oaktag and help you decide what to write on the paper. Hang in a row at eye level. You now have an event-time sequence board children can refer to whenever they wonder when it is time to go home.

3 Use time-related language to help children read the time line: "Now we are at circle time. What comes next? What do we do after that? What is the last activity we do?"

> **MATERIALS:** camera, oaktag, glue stick, markers
>
> **SKILLS:** sequencing, comparative analysis, temporal relationships

● As the year progresses, add the actual time (represented by clock face drawings) to the photo cards. Children can match the clock on the card to the one on the wall to know if it is time for a certain event yet!

Language & Literacy

Adjective Adventure

Explore the sound and joy of language. Most children are now comfortable enough to be able to participate fully in language games. And there's so much to say at this time of year!

HOW-TO

1 With children in a circle, share an interesting object. Invite children to observe the object silently. Ask, "What do you notice about this? How would you describe it to someone who can't see it? What words describe its size, color, shape, and texture?"

2 Begin the game by saying one adjective with the noun. For instance, if it is a new stuffed dog, "black dog." Invite children to say these words with you. Ask, "What other words can we use to describe it?" (*fluffy*). Add to the name and have the group repeat. Continue until you have a long line of descriptive adjectives for it (*fluffy, black, silly, funny, fat, big dog!*).

Using Chart Paper

Write down the descriptive adjectives as children suggest them.

MATERIALS: interesting object (something children have not seen in the room before)

SKILLS: speaking, listening, memorizing, descriptive language

- You might ask guiding questions, such as "Is it big or little?"

- Play a variation called "One More Thing." Use pictures from magazines or favorite books. Ask children to tell you what the picture shows (for instance, *it's a house*). Then ask them to tell one more thing about it (*it is yellow*). Keep adding one more way to describe it, until everyone who wants a turn has had one.

Our Songbook

December is the perfect time to make a class gift for children's families and friends.

HOW-TO

1. Discuss with children their favorite songs in school so far this year. What are they? Suggest that children choose several of their favorites to include in a songbook as a gift for their families.

2. Write the words to the songs and copy each page, leaving room for children to illustrate the pages. Suggest that children make covers, and help them bind them together so that each child has one book.

3. Set up your circle time area as a recording studio. Record children singing the songs on tape (they can refer to their books as they do so). Keep playing the tape back for children to listen to and approve!

MATERIALS: chart paper, drawing materials, tape recorder, blank tapes

SKILLS: listening, singing

Tips

- Put the tape in the classroom lending library for families to borrow.

- Take some photos of the recording project in action, and display them on your hallway bulletin board or add them to the take-home songbooks.

Using Chart Paper

- Have children list the titles of their favorite songs. Then ask them to vote for the ones they like best.

- Make big song charts for children to read independently.

Community Building

A Time of Giving

Sharing and helping are great ways to create a class community project. Children can choose a cause to support.

HOW-TO

1 Read a book about giving, such as *The Giving Tree*, by Shel Silverstein. Use the situation in the book to get a conversation going about giving and receiving. Ask, "What did the tree do whenever the boy needed something?" Elicit children's ideas about giving. Then ask, "What can we do to help people who need things? What do we have to offer?"

2 Together, brainstorm a list of ways children can help others during the holiday season (such as saving pennies or collecting clothes for a shelter).

3 Once the collection of offerings has grown, bring the items to circle time for a discussion. Count and tally each day the amount that has come in. Do this over a period of several weeks so that children can see the results of their efforts.

MATERIALS: small container to use as a piggy bank, large boxes for collecting clothing

SKILLS: counting, cooperation

● Children can also make pictures or cards for children in a local hospital or the elderly in a local nursing home.

Using Chart Paper

To encourage other members of the community to contribute, make a sign advertising the clothing or penny drive.

Rhythm Stick Syllables

With all the holiday excitement, this is a good time to do simple, comforting activities. Remember, children may need shorter circle times now!

HOW-TO

1 Give each child a pair of rhythm sticks and have one child sit in the center of the circle.

2 That child says his or her name while tapping out the syllables. The children in the circle listen first and then copy the pattern. How special it is to hear a circle of friends tapping your name!

3 After several times, the child in the center joins the circle and chooses someone to take his or her place.

MATERIALS: rhythm sticks (1 pair per child)

SKILLS: listening, counting, self-esteem

- Don't forget to include your name and the names of others in the school community!

- Have a child tap the syllables in a friend's name as the others guess whose name he or she is tapping!

- Determine whose name has the most and fewest syllables.

Sound Secrets

Sound activities offer practice in using listening and thinking skills, and they help children develop better focus.

HOW-TO

1 Before circle time, pass out paper bags and ask children to go on a sound hunt around the room. Their task is to find something that makes a sound and hide it in their bag.

2 At circle time, children can take turns going behind a shelf or screen to make their secret sound. Ask, "Can you guess the secret sound? What is it?" The child can give clues, such as "These are things we build with. What are they?" (*blocks*)

- ◉ Put all the objects together in a secret sound symphony! Sing a favorite song or play music and use the items as instruments.

- ◉ Give circle time "homework"! Ask children to bring in something from home that makes a sound.

- ◉ Make a tape recording of sounds around your home for children to guess at circle time. They will be fascinated to hear where the sounds came from. (Many children believe that teachers live at school!)

MATERIALS: small paper bags (1 per child)

SKILLS: listening, speaking, comparing, predicting

Using Chart Paper

Create a predictions and results chart for the game. Write children's secret sound speculations on one side of the chart and the results on another!

Toy Stories

No matter what the winter weather is, you can gather your group around an imaginary fire and tell stories together.

HOW-TO

1 Use toys for collective storytelling! Send home a note to families explaining that their child can bring in a toy to show on a particular day. (This activity works best if you have only a few children sharing at a time, so you might spread this activity out over several days.)

2 During circle time, ask children (one at a time) to hold up their toy, show it to the group, then put the toy in the box. Then say, "Now we can use our toys to make up a toy story. Don't worry, you will get your toy back at the end of circle time."

3 Reach in the gift box and pull out one toy. If the toy is a teddy bear, for instance, you might start the story by saying, "Once upon a time there was a little bear. He was happily walking along until, OOPS! He bumped into a…" Then pass the box to the child next to you and have him or her pull out a toy and use it to continue the story. When the box is empty, create an ending together.

Using Chart Paper

◉ Write the story on chart paper as children create it, and leave room on the page for children to add illustrations during choice time.

> **MATERIALS:** large, decorated box or bag, toys brought from home (supplemented by a few classroom favorites)
>
> **SKILLS:** expressive language, sequencing, creative thinking

◉ Some children may be quiet and shy at first. Ask questions such as "Who did he meet? What did he do?" If a child "freezes," you can use the toy yourself to keep the story moving.

◉ Tell winter stories using objects such as a mitten, hat, scarf, toy shovel, sled, even the makings for a snowman!

The Dance of the Snow People

What would happen if snow danced? How would it move?
Here's a great way to find out!

HOW-TO

1. Give children a paper doily to use as their own personal snowflake. Teach them a simple song to the tune of "I'm a Little Teapot":

   I'm a little snowflake, icy cold,
   White and frosty and shivery cold!
   When the air is wet and gray
   I float on down to you today.

2. Put on the music and ask children to move like a snowflake as they float their doily in the air. Invite children to whirl and spin like flakes do in the wind, while staying in the circle.

3. As they move, you can tell a story to inspire their movements:

   It was a cold, cold day and the snow was falling lightly.
   Big and small flakes gently floated to the ground.
   From the north, the wind appeared and swept the flakes
   back into the air. The snow scattered about and floated
   up and down as the wind blew harder and harder. All of
   a sudden a giant gust of wind blew the snowflakes into
   a circle, and they spun around and around to its
   howling sounds. But not for long, because the wind
   shifted and slowed down as the sun came out. The little
   flakes, tired from their adventure, floated back to the
   ground and, feeling the warmth of the sun, melted into
   the earth.

MATERIALS: paper doilies (1 per child) with a 2-foot piece of string taped to each, recorded "wintry" music for movement (such as "Winter" from Vivaldi's *Four Seasons*)

SKILLS: creative expression, gross motor, listening

Using Chart Paper

Create a class snow poem. On a sheet of chart paper, draw the intersecting lines of a simple snowflake (be sure to leave room to write on the lines). Ask children to suggest different words to describe snow (such as *wet, cold, slippery, puffy*) and write the words on the lines of the snowflake. Title the poem: "Snow Is…" and read it aloud!

Collective Storytelling

Once you help them get started, most children have no trouble making up a story. Best of all, when children collaborate on a story or poem, they are less likely to feel shy or put on the spot.

There are several ways to do collective storytelling:

⊙ Read aloud an unfamiliar book and stop at a climactic point in the story. Invite children to suggest what would happen next. Write their ideas on chart paper, and then vote for their favorite! Great books to finish are: *Cloudy With a Chance of Meatballs*, by Judi Barrette; *Caps for Sale*, by Esphyr Slobodkina; and *Inside a Zoo in the City*, by Alyssa Satin Capucilli.

⊙ Start with a thought-provoking sentence starter, encouraging children to finish it. Good starters are:

"On my street…," "When my grandparents visited…," "I hate it when…."

⊙ Create a poem together based on a repeating pattern, such as:

In the cold dark woods there is a cold dark cliff.

In the cold dark cliff there is a cold dark cave.

In the cold dark cave there is a cold dark [next item, and so on]

End with:

"In the cold dark _____ there is a _____ looking at me!"

Use your best scary voice! Then ask children to suggest what they might find in the cold dark woods. Add their suggestions to the poem, and keep reading!

> **MATERIALS:** chart paper, markers, storybook
>
> **SKILLS:** cooperation, expressive language

⊙ Pass around a rock, ball, or other favorite object as children take turns speaking. Remind children that whoever is holding the object is the only one speaking.

 Math

Story Problems

How is math like a story? When it is a story problem!
Children can count back and forth to help you tell a story.

HOW-TO

1 Have six children act out a story in the middle of the circle. Give children hats, masks, or props to add to the fun as you read the following story aloud:

> *Four little snowmen were sitting in a field. Along came a crow and knocked a snowman down. (A child pretends to fly in and gently pushes one over.) Now how many are left? (3) Along comes a little girl. She builds the snowman back up and makes one more. Now how many snowmen? (5) As the day goes by the sun comes out and warms the snowmen. Slowly, slowly they all melt away. How many snowmen are there now? (0!)*

2 Have children suggest other stories and act those out. You might give one child a simple story idea and have him or her narrate.

MATERIALS: none

SKILLS: counting, adding, subtracting, following directions

 Tip

⊙ Take your time while telling the story, giving children plenty of time to act and react to the story.

Using Chart Paper

Invite children to use tally marks to represent the number of snowmen. Keep a running tally of the number of snowmen until there are none. If possible, have children write the numerals as well.

Shadow Plays

As the light changes in the winter, so do the shadows, making a perfect topic for circle time science!

HOW-TO

1 On a sunny day, invite children to look around the room for shadows (shadows can be made by overhead lights as well as the sun). Ask, "Where do you see shadows in the room? What do you think is creating them? If we move the object that is casting a shadow, will the shadow move, too?"

2 Bring out some objects and allow children to experiment with flashlights to create a shadow. Children can also create hand shadows.

3 Now you are ready to create a shadow play! Invite children to choose several objects and to tell a story (you might start off with a favorite puppet or doll). Have children go behind the sheet and create the shadows with the flashlight as they tell a story.

MATERIALS: interestingly shaped objects, old sheet, flashlights

SKILLS: observing, predicting, experimenting

Tips

◉ While holding an object behind a sheet, shine the flashlight on it. What is it? You can do this with classroom objects, letter shapes, or children's show-and-tell items.

◉ Use mural paper and a flashlight to create shadow tracings. Children can pair up and take turns tracing and then coloring each other's shadows.

Using Chart Paper

Create a shadow chart. Starting at circle time, and continuing throughout the day, invite children to watch the shadows in the room change. Choose a big shadow by the window to measure with a piece of yarn or string. Write the time and length of the shadow on the chart. A while later, measure the shadow again with another piece of yarn. Write this measurement on the chart next to the current time. Is the shadow getting longer or shorter?

Language & Literacy

Tell Me a Superlative

Introduce the concept of superlatives at circle time.

HOW-TO

1 Tell the story of The Three Bears. As you tell the story, emphasize the "biggest" bowl, the "biggest" chair, and the "biggest" bed. Then invite children to think of examples of other superlative words, such as *smallest, fastest, slowest, funniest, silliest, ugliest,* and *yuckiest.*

2 Give children a sentence to finish, such as "The biggest thing in the whole wide world is…." Write children's ideas on chart paper.

3 Focus on the -est ending of superlative words. Make a list of fun superlative words, drawing children's attention to the word endings. Ask, "What do you notice about these words? How are they the same? How are they different?" Help children see that adding the ending -est to a descriptive word creates a superlative.

MATERIALS: chart paper, marker, story that demonstrates superlative language (for example, The Three Bears)

SKILLS: expressive and receptive language, listening, creative thinking, writing

⊙ Read some books about the biggest, reddest dog ever, Clifford the Big Red Dog!

Give Your Heart Away!

This is a great month to talk about sharing feelings with family and friends.

HOW-TO

1 Ask children to tell about the ways they like to show people that they love them. You might mention that making valentines is one way people do this.

2 Teach children this song, to the tune of "Skip to My Lou." Ask children to listen to the song a few times and then join in when they feel comfortable.

Valen-tine, red, pink, and blue,
Here's a nice one from me to you.
Valen-tine, red, green, too,
Here's one more from me to you.

3 Now show the decorated container of hearts and have each child choose one to start with. Start the song again and encourage children to pass the hearts around the circle, like the game of hot potato. Stop passing when the music stops. Invite children to look at the heart they are now holding. Is it the same color or a different color this time? Repeat, changing the direction of the passing now and then.

4 When the game is over, children keep the hearts they are holding. They might decorate them before taking them home.

MATERIALS: paper hearts in different colors (1 per child), container decorated for Valentine's Day

SKILLS: fine and gross motor, cooperation, rhythm, singing

● You can use this game with any seasonal topic. Just cut seasonal shapes and make up new words to the song!

Using Chart Paper

Here is another song to sing with this activity. Write the words on chart paper so that children can follow along as they sing.

Love is something
if you give it away,
Give it away, give it away.
Love is something
if you give it away,
You end up having more.

Community Building

The Longest Paper Chain Ever

Paper chains are great decorations for a Valentine's Day party! Invite children to start working on a paper chain at circle time.

HOW-TO

 Ask children, "If we all worked together, could we make the longest paper chain ever? How long a chain do you think you can make? Would it be as long as the circle time area rug? The room? The hall? The whole school?"

2 Pass out several strips of paper for each child. Demonstrate how to curl the strips into a circle and fasten. Then thread the next strip through the circle and fasten. Children can work on their own part of the chain as you carry on with your usual circle time activities.

3 Sing a song to the tune of "Here We Go 'Round the Mulberry Bush" as you work.

Around and around and around we go,
Making little circles in a row.
Around and around and around we go,
The longest chain ever so!

MATERIALS: paper strips (in various colors, or red, pink, and white for Valentine's Day), tape or stapler

SKILLS: cooperation, fine motor, predicting

- Use double-sided tape for easier fastening.
- Invite children to create color patterns in the chain.

Will It Fit?

Children often love the boxes presents come in just as much as what's inside! Use boxes to play some size comparison games at circle time.

HOW-TO

1 Spread out the separated boxes and lids in the center of your circle. Show one box and ask, "Who can find the lid that fits this box?" Then give each child a box or lid and ask children to look around the circle to see who has the box that fits their lid (or vice versa). Go around the circle and have each child identify their match. The children with boxes then take the lids and put them on the boxes.

2 Next, focus on objects that can fit in the boxes. You might ask, "Can someone find an object that just fits inside this box? Let's try it and see!" This time, give the children who are not holding boxes the objects and have them identify whose box it might fit into.

> **MATERIALS:** various boxes with matching lids, objects that just fit inside each
>
> **SKILLS:** sorting, matching, comparing, fine motor

Tips

- Invite children to help you put the boxes in size order. Invite children to suggest words for the gradations of sizes. The smallest could be *teeny tiny*, the next *tiny*, the next *little*, and so forth, up to the biggest box!

- Play music and have children stand in two concentric circles facing each other (boxes on the outside, lids on the inside). When the music plays, they move around the circle. When the music stops, they face a friend and see if their box and lid fit!

- Hide things inside the boxes and invite children to guess what is inside, based on the sound it makes.

Sprouting Seeds

Growth and change are a basic part of children's lives.
Try sprouting mung or lima beans indoors! When soaked in water,
these little beans will sprout and grow quickly.

HOW-TO

1. Bring the beans to circle time and give one to each child to examine. Encourage children to predict what the bean might grow into. "How big do you think the plant from this bean will grow? Can you show me with your hands?"

2. Bring a dishpan of water to the circle and place it on a plastic tablecloth in the center of the circle. Children can take turns scooping water out of the dishpan into their cup. Then they can place their beans (several, in case some do not sprout) in the cup to soak overnight. (Write children's initials on the cups.)

3. The next day, pour out the water, take out a bean, and observe it. How has it changed? Place a damp paper towel inside the cup and put the beans back in. Top the cups with more paper towels and place near your meeting area. Observe the seeds each day to observe their growth. How much bigger will they get?

MATERIALS: plastic tablecloth, dishpan of water, clear plastic cups (1 per child), mung or lima beans (several per child), paper towels

SKILLS: predicting, observing

- Make it a growing race! Choose a variety of beans and seeds to sprout and grow, and watch to see which gets biggest the fastest. Invite children to make predictions, and write them on chart paper. After a period of time, show the results. Which bean won?

- A sweet potato grows a vine very quickly when suspended in water. You can also start sunflower or marigold seeds for later spring planting.

What Makes the Wind?

March comes in like a lion, but *you* can start off the month with this discussion and creative writing activity.

HOW-TO

 Copy the following poem onto chart paper and read it with children:

Who Has Seen the Wind?

Who has seen the wind?
  Neither I nor you:
But when the leaves hang trembling,
  The wind is passing through

Who has seen the wind?
  Neither you nor I:
But when the trees bow down their heads,
  The wind is passing by.
              —Christina Rossetti

 Ask, "How do you know when the wind is blowing? Can you see the wind?" Although it is difficult to actually see the wind, we can see the effects of it: how it moves things, and, in storms, how it damages trees and property. Invite children to share experiences they have had with the wind.

After all this windy discussion, you are ready for the creative thinking question! Ask children, "Where does wind come from? What makes the wind?" Tell children there is no right or wrong answer, that this is an opportunity for them to think creatively. As children suggest their ideas, write them on chart paper with the child's name. (You will probably hear everything from "little spacemen are blowing from the clouds" to "a giant fan in the sky," so be prepared for some fun creative thinking!)

MATERIALS: chart paper, markers

SKILLS: expressive and creative language and writing skills

TIPS

⊙ This activity is best done on a windy day so that children can actually observe the wind outside.

⊙ Extend the activity by making wind paintings. Put out thinned-out tempera paint, paper, and straws. Children put a blob of paint on their paper and blow on it with a straw!

42

Music & Movement

Bubbles in the Wind

In good weather, this a wonderful activity to bring outside
for a windy day circle time.

HOW-TO

1 Provide children each with a paper streamer to
hold as they stand up in the circle. Ask, "Is the
wind blowing? How do you know? How can you
move and dance with the wind? How does it make
you want to move?" If you have a tape player, play
some music as children move.

2 Blow a few bubbles into the middle of the circle
and invite children to watch their movements.
Do they move fast or slow? What happens when the
wind blows?

3 Time to move around some more! Suggest that
children pretend to be bubbles. "How would
you move if you were a bubble?" To add some fun
and drama to the dance, use a hula hoop as a giant
bubble wand! Put on music and ask children one at a
time to pass through the wand and float away as a
bubble! Ask them to think about what their bodies
would look like if they were big round bubbles.

4 Ask, "What happens when if two bubbles
touch?" (They pop or join together and slowly
float to the ground.) Invite children to be "touching
bubbles" and float down to the ground and melt
away.

MATERIALS: paper
streamers, bubble wands
and soapy water, hula hoop

SKILLS: creative movement
and expression, fine motor,
gross motor

● Write the following song on
chart paper for children to
read! Sing to the tune of "Sing
a Song of Sixpence":

Sing a Song of Bubbles
Floating in the air.
Filled with rainbow colors
Swirling here and there.
As I blow my bubbles,
I don't want to stop.
What fun it is to catch one,
And touch it with a POP!

The Classroom News

Once children start sharing, it's often hard to get them to stop! Turn to the newspaper for structure and help—it's a great way for children to practice collaboration.

HOW-TO

1 Bring in a few different newspapers to show children. Show and read the headlines (of course, choose headlines appropriate for children). Ask children to guess what the story is about, based on the headline. Point out that headlines are just short phrases that tell a lot!

2 Next time children want to share something with the group, have them say their "news" as headlines. Show children a pretty stone or stick. Explain that it is a "talking" stone or stick, and whoever is holding it is the only one talking. Remind children to share just one thought or phrase.

3 Pass the stone or stick around the circle, giving each child a chance to share his or her headline.

Using Chart Paper

Make a list of children's headlines.

MATERIALS: newspapers, chart paper, markers, stone or stick

SKILLS: creative expression, cooperative thinking, collaboration

Tips

● Don't worry if children take time learning to distill their thoughts into one statement. You can help them by showing them when and how to stop!

● Create a class newspaper out of the headlines. This can be an engaging weeklong project. During choice time, children can take their headlines from the chart and add their own drawings, writing, and dictation. At the end of the week, read the newspaper aloud.

 Math

Marching Math Madness!

All the spring wind in the air makes children just want to get up and move!

HOW-TO

1 Have children go around the circle and count off by twos (1-2-1-2-1-2). To help children remember which number they are, have the ones stand up. Then ask the ones to sit down and the twos to stand up.

2 Use the song "The Ants Go Marching" to practice counting by ones and twos. Sing the song through a few times:

The ants go marching one by one, Hoorah, Hoorah.
The ants go marching one by one, Hoorah, Hoorah.
The ants go marching one by one,
  the little one stops to suck his thumb.
And they all go marching down into the ground
  to get out of the rain, boom boom boom!

The ants go marching two by two, Hoorah, Hoorah.
The ants go marching two by two, Hoorah, Hoorah.
The ants go marching two by two,
  the little one stops to tie his shoe.
And they all go marching down into the ground
  to get out of the rain, boom boom boom!

3 Time to march! Invite all the ones to stand up and march around the circle as the first verse is sung. During the second verse, the ones find a two partner to march with. At the end, have children stop, hold hands to form a circle, and count off by twos.

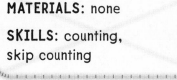

MATERIALS: none

SKILLS: counting, skip counting

Tips

- Don't forget to choose someone to be the "little one" at the end of the line!

- With practice, children will get better and better at this type of counting.

- After they have mastered counting by twos, try threes and add a verse to the song ("The ants go marching three by three, the little one stopped to tap his knee").

Blowing in the Wind

Invite children to be "wind scientists."

HOW-TO

1. Ask children, "Can you make air move like the wind?" Show them how they can blow on their hands and feel the air move just like the wind! Ask, "How many different ways can you move the air? Who can show me one?" Encourage children to create moving air with their breath, their hands, or by using a piece of paper as a fan.

2. Tell children that as wind scientists, their task is to predict and test the power of wind by using the different objects in the center of the circle. Ask children to predict which items they think they can move just by blowing with their breath. Let children come to the center of the circle and take turns trying to blow away or move each of the objects. If one child can't move it, can two or more? Encourage them to try blowing from different angles.

3. Have children change the way they create the wind. If they can't move an object by blowing on it through their mouth alone, what would happen if they used a straw? Pass out straws and allow children to experience the difference when the column of air is more focused!

MATERIALS: small objects (toy cars, balls, scrap paper, rocks, books, fabric pieces, spools, yarn, paper, markers), disposable straws

SKILLS: observing, predicting, experimenting, problem solving

TIP

⊙ Invite children to suggest items in the room they can use to create more wind power.

What's in the Bag?

Here's a playful, word-oriented guessing game in which children use both their sense of touch and their knowledge of descriptive words.

HOW-TO

1 Tell children they will be reaching inside a bag and describing what they feel. Bring the bag out with the stuffed animal hidden inside. Label a chart "How Does It Feel?" Halfway down, write "What Do You Think It Is?" If children think they know what the mystery object is, tell them to keep their guesses to themselves until everyone has had a turn.

2 Pass the bag to the first child and ask him or her to use one word to describe how it feels. You might ask questions, such as "Is it big? Little? Soft? Bumpy? Round? What can you tell me about the way it feels?" Write children's words or phrases on the chart.

3 After the bag has been passed around the circle, read the adjectives together. Now it's time for children to make their guesses! Write down each child's guess. With a dramatic flair, say *Voila!* and whip out the object.

MATERIALS: familiar object such as a puppet or stuffed animal, large paper bag loosely tied at the top (so that only a small hand and arm can slip through without the object inside being seen), chart paper and marker

SKILLS: expressive language, observation, predicting

- Extend this activity by using the rich collection of child-generated adjectives in a class poem or story.

- Have children choose a descriptive word from the chart and an object that fits its description to complete the sentence "My _____ is _____."

Little Seeds

Young children love to pretend—and they are good at it!

HOW-TO

Play soft music, use a quiet voice and tell children the following story as they act it out:

> Pretend that you are a tiny seed way down in the ground. You have been sleeping all winter. (Roll your body into a ball and lie very still.) All of a sudden the ground around you starts to get warm and you start to wiggle just a little. (wiggle toes) As you get warmer you start to move a little more. (wiggle toes and feet) And a little more. The dirt around you feels damp now, and you can hear the rain above you. (Hold your hand to your ear as if you are listening.) Tiny roots begin to grow out of you at the bottom and a little stem grows up. (Sit up in a crouching position with hands at sides pointing up.) Your stem gets a little taller and soon you have leaves (Stand up slowly with hands still at sides, but pointing out with fingers spread apart.) The sun is shining on you and a tiny bud appears on the stem. (Bring hands together as if you are holding something inside.) You grow a little taller and POOF! the bud opens into a beautiful flower. (Open your hands, make a big circle with them above your head, and smile.)

MATERIALS: soft music

SKILLS: creative movement and expression, gross motor, listening

Using Chart Paper

- Have children draw and label the parts of a plant.

- Make a group collage of flowers or plants cut from magazines.

Music & Movement

Clap, Clap, Clap

If children are antsy and need a break, try this!

HOW-TO

1. Tell children to follow your movements as you chant and do the following:

   Clap, clap, clap.
   Lean to the left,
   Lean to the right,
   Stand up, sit down,
   Clap, clap, clap.

2. Substitute other actions for "stand up, sit down," such as "lean forward, lean backward" or "nod yes, nod no," and have children listen carefully for the different instructions.

3. Continue until children are engaged and focused.

MATERIALS: none

SKILLS: listening, gross motor, directionality

 Tips

- Substitute *snap* for *clap*.

- Invite children to go for a swim with you! Model the crawl stroke, and have children count to ten as they imitate you with ten strokes. Repeat, imitating the breaststroke and sidestroke.

A Web of Greeting

Learning to work together is an important skill for children to learn. This activity demonstrates the necessity of working together to achieve a common goal.

HOW-TO

1 With children in a circle, tell them that they will be greeting their classmates in a new and fun way. Choose one child to help you model the following greeting:

> Teacher: Hello, [child's name], how are you?
>
> Child: I'm fine [or any other adjective], thank you, and how are you?
>
> Teacher: I'm fine, thanks.

2 Practice until you are confident everyone can say the greeting. Next, show children the ball of string and say, "If everyone works together we can spin a beautiful spider web." Tell them that it is important to hold their part of the string and not let it go. Emphasize how you are holding a piece of the string in one hand and the ball of string in the other.

3 Choose a child and say, "Hello, [child's name]. How are you?" and hand the child the string. He or she takes the string and says, "I'm fine, thank you, and how are you?" You smile and say, "I'm fine, thanks." That child then chooses another child, greets him or her, then, holding tight to one end of the string, hands the ball to the child he or she has just greeted.

4 Proceed until everyone has been greeted and children have created a beautiful web!

MATERIALS: ball of string

SKILLS: cooperation, collaboration, gross motor

- Remind children to hold the string tight and not let go!

- If you have another adult in the room, have him or her walk around the outside of the circle, helping and reminding children what to do.

Using Chart Paper

Make a three-column K-W-L chart: What We Know, What We Want to Know, What We Learned. Ask children what they know about spiders, and record what they say on a chart. Ask them what they would like to know about spiders. Then share nonfiction books about spiders, and record what you've learned.

Math

Counting Down

Count down to the last day of school, and build math skills at the same time!

HOW-TO

1 Display the number line when there are 100 days of school remaining. Each day, cut one numeral off the number line and say, for instance: "There are 100 days left to be together in school, so each day we will cut off one day to keep track of the days left. If there are 100 days and we take one away, how many days are left? Who can think of a number sentence to tell what we did?" Elicit that 100 minus one leaves 99. Show children how to write the equation using numerals $(100 - 1 = 99)$.

2 Do this every day, and soon children will be volunteering the number sentence and writing the equation with ease.

Tips

⦿ Create a number line with numerals equaling the number of children in the group. Designate one child to start the activity. As you point to him or her, he or she says "one." Next, point to the number two and the person sitting to the right of the "starter" will say "two," and so on around the circle, until you get back to the starter. When you are finished counting off, let children figure out if anyone is absent. Ask for a volunteer to tell you a number story for the attendance, such as "We usually have 20 kids, but today we only have 19 because [child's name] is absent."

⦿ Ask children who speak other languages to play "teacher" and teach the group to count off in their language. Invite parents in to be teachers as well.

MATERIALS: number line made from cash register tape, marker, scissors

SKILLS: counting, numeration

Using Chart Paper

List the numbers 1 to 100 on chart paper. Randomly choose a number and have children count backward or forward to the number you point to. Make it tricky—tell them to start at 87 and count backward until they get to 79, or start at 29 and count forward until they get to 42. Ask for volunteers to point to the numbers.

Wake Up, Earth!

In many regions of the country, as April rolls around and winter comes to an end, the earth starts to wake up. Birds return, insects buzz, and the air starts to feel warmer.

HOW-TO

1 Say, "Let's do a little experiment to see if we can trick the earth into waking up any sooner!" Go for a walk outside and find a piece of ground that is easy to dig up. Dig up some earth and put it into the tank to bring inside. Place it in the center of your circle and ask, "What do you see?" Record all observations on a chart.

2 Have a discussion about what living things need in order to grow. Accept all comments, but elicit that living things need warmth, sunlight, air, and water. Ask, "If we give this earth lots of light, air, warmth and water, do you think things will begin to grow? Those who think yes, stand up. Those who think no, remain seated." Count each group, and record results.

3 Ask, "What do you think will grow?" Write down all predictions. Leave a space on the chart labeled "What actually grew?" Place the tank on the looking table and observe and comment on it daily during circle time, recording anything that grows. Things become exciting as grass, weeds, and flowers begin to grow—and children can't wait to see what grows next.

MATERIALS: shovel, small fish tank, chart paper, marker

SKILLS: observation, prediction, experimentation

- Play soft music and invite children to dance around the circle doing a "Wake Up the Earth" dance. Encourage children to imitate rain, warmth, sunshine, air, baby plants, and so on.

Language & Literacy

Class Yearbook

If "big kids" can have a yearbook, so can your little ones!
As the year starts to wind down, a yearbook is a great ongoing circle time activity to celebrate each child.

HOW-TO

1 Using chart paper and the simple format of "five-step poetry," children can work over the next month to create a page in the yearbook for each child. Do just one or two children at each circle time throughout the month.

2 Invite the child as well as the class to make suggestions for the words in each step. The five steps are:

* Child's name   (Maya)
* Two descriptive words   (Colorful, beautiful)
* Three favorite classroom   (Playing, reading, snacking) activities
* A phrase the child wants   (Proud of myself) to say about him or herself
* The child's name again.   (Maya)

3 Copy each child's poem onto a sheet of drawing paper (or type it on the computer and print it out). Have children add their self-portrait to their page. Collect the pages and photocopy and bind together a complete set for each child. Each child can create his or her own cover!

MATERIALS: chart paper, markers, white drawing paper, crayons, and markers Optional: computer and printer

SKILLS: expressive vocabulary, creative writing, self-concept

May Day

May Day has been celebrated for centuries and signals the beginning of spring. In England, on the morning of the first of May, a tree was brought into town, decorated with flowers and streamers, and danced around.

HOW-TO

1 Take circle time outside. Find a tree or basketball pole and tape crepe paper streamers (one per child) to the top of it.

2 Have children gather in a circle, with lively music playing. Each child holds a streamer and skips to the right ten times. Invite them to look up and observe the beautiful pattern they have created with their crepe paper.

3 Then, they skip to the left ten times to undo the pattern. Prepare yourself for cries of "one more time!"

MATERIALS: crepe paper strips in different colors, strong tape

SKILLS: creative movement, gross motor, cooperation

● Children can write "Happy May Day" cards to take home to someone special.

Community Building

Pass the Hula Hoop

Working together in a noncompetitive way to reach a common goal fosters a sense of community and accomplishment.

HOW-TO

1 Invite children to stand in a circle and hold hands. Put your arm through the center of a hula hoop and hold the hand of the child next to you.

2 Tell children that the object of the game is to pass the hoop from one person to the next around the circle without dropping hands. It CAN be done with cooperation! Start the passing of the hoop, to demonstrate one way of successfully passing it along (there are many different ways).

3 Congratulate children when they get it all the way around the circle!

MATERIALS: hula hoop

SKILLS: gross motor, creative movement, cooperation

- Be prepared for everyone to talk at once as they make suggestions about how to move the hula hoop.

- If it gets too noisy to hear children's suggestions, invite them to sit down and take a break to brainstorm ideas before going back and trying them again.

Bounce and Count

Here is a fun game that gives children practice in counting, active listening, hand-eye coordination, and gross-motor agility.

HOW-TO

1 One child in the circle starts the game. He or she secretly chooses a number between one and ten and uses two hands to bounce the ball that number of times. The rest of the children in the circle listen carefully and count the number of bounces silently to themselves.

2 The bouncer calls on a volunteer to tell how many bounces he or she heard. If the guess is incorrect, the bouncer calls on other volunteers until the number is guessed correctly. The child who guesses correctly becomes the bouncer and the game repeats.

> **MATERIALS:** ball
>
> **SKILLS:** listening, numeration, counting, gross motor

Tips

- Raise or lower the maximum number of bounces, depending on the comfort level of the group.

- To add a challenge to the game, have the "guesser" clap the number of bounces, without saying the numbers out loud.

Math

Teddy Bear Number Stories

Using real materials helps children visualize difficult concepts. The following activity can introduce many different mathematical ideas.

HOW-TO

1 Give chicken each a tree page and five teddy bear counters. Have them place everything in front of them. Tell children that you will be telling a number story and asking them questions, and they can act out the stories with their teddy bear counters.

2 Read the following story and stop to let children answer the questions:

One day five teddy bear friends go for a walk in the forest. One decides to climb the biggest tree. *"How many are still on the ground?"* The one in the tree yells "Come on up!" *"If two teddy bears climb up the tree, then how many are still on the ground? How many are up in the tree? How many are there all together?"* A teddy bear on the ground says, "That tree is too scary, I'm going to climb the medium-sized one," and he does. *"If two are on the ground and one climbs a tree, how many are left on the ground? How many teddy bears are in the biggest tree? In the medium sized tree? In the smallest tree? On the ground? All together?"* The teddy bear in the medium sized tree says "This is no fun, I'm going home," and he does. There were five teddy bears and one went home. *"How many are left in the forest? In the medium sized tree? In the biggest tree? On the ground?"*

MATERIALS: teddy bear counters (5 per child), simple drawing of a large, medium, and small tree (1 copy per child)

SKILLS: counting, addition, subtraction

● Let children add to the story or make up a new story problem.

Time for Trees!

Explore a forest habitat. If you do not have access to a forest, a tree and creative thinking will do!

HOW-TO

1 Draw a tree on chart paper and ask children to help you label its parts (roots, trunk, bark, leaves, branches, fruit). Explain that each part of a tree has an important function and is dependent upon all other parts to thrive. Ask children to tell you what they know about the different parts of a tree, eliciting the following: A tree is a giant plant. The roots take in nourishment and secure the tree in the ground. The trunk holds the branches, which in turn holds the leaves and fruit. The bark protects the trunk. The leaves and the sun make food for the tree. Keep it simple, stressing how all parts work together as a team just as you do in your class.

2 Go for a walk to observe a tree and find all the parts you have been discussing. Help focus children by asking questions about how the tree looks, feels, and sounds.

3 Back in the circle, record all observations on chart paper. You might also discuss ways that trees help people: by keeping the air clean; giving us oxygen to breathe and food to eat, providing wood for paper; furniture, and homes; giving us shade, and so on.

MATERIALS: chart paper, markers

SKILLS: observation

● Have children draw their own tree and label the parts.

Write the following song on chart paper to read, sing, and act out. Sing to the tune of "I'm a Little Teapot"!

I'm a little tree,
(stand tall with arms stretched out)

Come look at me.
(wiggle fingers)

I make oxygen

For you and me.
(blow out and breathe in)

If you get hot, then
(drag right hand across forehead)

You have it made.

Come by me
(one hand beckoning signal)

And get some shade!
(arms stretched out and swinging)

A Message for the Future

June is a time for reflecting and looking back on a busy year.

HOW-TO

 Ask children if they remember how they felt on the first day of school, and tell them that you need their help in writing a message to the incoming class so they won't be nervous! Tell them to close their eyes and think about what they liked best this year. When they are ready to open their eyes, you will write down what they say on chart paper. You might start the message.

 Compose a whole letter, such as:

Dear New Students,
We would like to tell you about the fun things that you will do in [teacher's name]'s class.
Johnny liked working on the computer.
Brittany liked dressing up in the house corner.
Morgan liked exploring at the water table.
Jessica liked creating in the art corner.
Jimmy liked learning to read (and so on).

From, (have all children sign their names)

You might also have children complete sentences such as "Here are some things to remember in [teacher's name]'s class…" or "The beginning of the year is fun because…."

 Put this in a safe place and use it on the first day of school at your very first circle time!

MATERIALS: chart paper, markers

SKILLS: reflection, self-awareness, expressive language

Tips

◉ Place a class picture at the bottom of the message.

◉ Have children illustrate the borders.

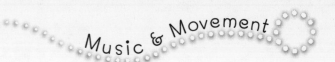

One More Time!

Children often regress to some earlier behaviors at this point in the year. With change looming in the future, they often want to go back a few steps to younger days and familiar things. So why not do just that?

HOW-TO

1 Challenge children to name all the songs they know! Invite children to suggest which ones they want to sing, and make a list on chart paper. Then sing them one by one.

2 Put the tape recorder in the center of the circle and tape children singing. Then play it back to them! If you made a tape earlier in the year for holiday gifts (see page 28), compare them. Ask, "How do we sound now? How is the recording the same or different?"

MATERIALS: chart paper, markers, tape recorder, blank tape

SKILLS: listening, speaking, singing

● Make a class phone book (with families' permission). On the first page, you can include a new song (sung to the tune of "We're Going to Kentucky"):

We're going on vacation.
We're going to go home.
We'll miss our friends at school,
But we'll call them on the phone.

Oh, dial it, dial it, dial it,
Dial it if you can.
Or get someone to help you—
Keep your friends close at hand!

Community Building

Kids' Choice Awards

Children can reminisce about the year and then create
their own awards for the "best of" the year!

HOW-TO

1 Ask children, "What were your favorite books,
games, songs, trips, poems, snacks, art
activities?" (Choose one category per day.) Make a
list of their responses on chart paper. Then have them
vote, tally the votes, and announce the winner.

2 Once you've voted in every category, have an
awards show! Children can dress up and arrive
on the "red carpet" (butcher paper that children have
painted, fingerpainted, or colored red) and
participate in a celebration of the winner of each
category. Read the book, sing the song, say the
poem—and don't forget to serve the favorite snack at
the post-awards show party!

MATERIALS: chart paper,
marker, white butcher
paper, and red paint,
fingerpaint, or crayons

SKILLS: collaborative
thinking, communication skills,
memory

- Children might share their
favorites in a simple
performance for parents.
Create handmade invitations
to send home for the special
show of their favorite songs,
poems, stories, and so on. Set
up a hallway art show of
children's favorite artwork, too.

Math

Growing Up

Part of growing up is facing the unknown...next year's class!
Children may be feeling a bit anxious about the change.
One way to face the future is to talk about the past.

HOW-TO

1 In advance, have children bring in clothing or shoes from the beginning of the school year. Have children lay their clothing or shoes in front of them in the circle.

2 Ask, "How have we grown this year? Are you bigger than at the beginning of the year? Does your clothing fit now? Is it too tight or short? Why?" It is helpful to have children lay the old piece of clothing over the new for them to see the difference.

3 If you made hand or footprints or height charts at the beginning of the year, bring them out and share them with the group.

MATERIALS: children's clothing or shoes from the beginning of the school year

SKILLS: reflection, comparison

TIPS

● You might ask, "How did you feel on the first day of school this year? What can you do now that you couldn't do then?"

● Pass around pictures from the beginning of the school year and ask children to notice some differences between then and now.

Counting Down

How many days until summer vacation? Let's count down and see!

HOW-TO

1 Invite children to make a summer vacation countdown chain out of construction paper (one link for each day). Hang it in your circle time area and have a child remove one each day. How many are left?

2 Next, have them sing the countdown to tune of "Ninety Nine Bottles of Pop on the Wall"! Always start at the top number and work down to the number for the day.

Twenty eight days until summertime,
Twenty eight days to go,
When one of those days is over and gone,
Twenty-seven days to go!

MATERIALS: construction paper cut into strips, glue sticks

SKILLS: comparative analysis, counting backward

Using Chart Paper

Create a countdown chart. Have children draw and paste pictures on a mural of their favorite summer activities. Starting on the first day of the month, count how many days until the last day of school and the beginning of vacation. Write the numerals (from 1 to the correct number) on a sheet of chart paper for children to copy. Ask a few children to write the numerals on sticky notes or squares of paper and hide them all over the mural (much like an advent calendar)! As the days progress, children take the highest number off the chart as they count down to vacation.

Notes